The Lost World

Arthur Conan Doyle

Adapted by Susan Gates

Illustrated by Mark Beech

Contents

Chapter 1: The scoop of the century   5

Chapter 2: The expedition begins   15

Chapter 3: Into the unknown   21

Chapter 4: A bridge to the lost world   30

Chapter 5: From a dream to a nightmare   39

Chapter 6: In deadly peril   50

Chapter 7: A midnight adventure   59

Chapter 8: Prisoners   67

Chapter 9: A tunnel to freedom   76

Chapter 10: Show us your proof!   85

CHAPTER I

The scoop of the century

'I need adventure!' I cried to Mr McArdle. 'Send me on a dangerous mission. I don't care what it is!'

Mr McArdle looked puzzled, or pretended to. 'Tut, tut,' he said. 'What is wrong with reporting flower shows and weddings?'

'But Mr McArdle, I'm *never* going to be famous that way. I want some big news to report. I want the scoop* of the century!'

Perhaps I ought to introduce myself. Edward D Malone at your service. I'm a junior reporter for the *London Daily Gazette*. And Mr McArdle is my news editor.

'You young men are so reckless, so hot-headed,' he said. 'Hmm. Now where could we send you?'

'I don't care where I go!' I cried. 'The more dangerous the better.'

'Very well,' said Mr McArdle, with a sly smile. 'I'll think about it.'

As I waited, my heart pounded. What faraway places would he send me to? What great adventures lay in store?

At last he spoke. 'You can go to the Zoological* Institute Hall at 8.30 tonight and report on a scientific meeting.'

It wasn't at all what I was expecting. My heart plunged down to my boots.

'Report on a scientific meeting?' I repeated. 'Here in London? That's not risking my life!'

'Don't be so sure,' said Mr McArdle. 'The great Professor Challenger is speaking. And he hates journalists. He once threw one down the stairs.'

I perked up again immediately.

'Professor Challenger!' I exclaimed. 'The man who says he found some kind of lost world in South America? With strange and marvellous creatures in it?'

'That's him,' said Mr McArdle. 'It's all nonsense, of course, this lost world stuff. The fellow's a shameless liar. So I want you to be at this meeting, where he'll be shown up as the fraud he is!'

So that's how I found myself, that night, with my reporter's notebook open, waiting eagerly for the famous professor to arrive.

No one had a good word to say for Professor Challenger. 'Stubborn', 'rude' and 'a big bully' were just a few of the things I heard about him. He was violent too. It wasn't only journalists he attacked. If *anyone* disagreed with him, he'd say, 'Come outside and fight!'

'He'd better not try that with me,' I muttered. 'He might get more than he bargained for.' I don't like to brag but I keep myself pretty fit. At school I was in the boxing team.

The audience around me were getting rowdy. They couldn't wait for the professor to arrive. They knew that soon sparks would be flying.

'Where is he?' yelled the crowd of students at the back. 'We want Professor Challenger!'

The professors at the front sat more quietly.

But I could see they were eager too. Eager to prove the famous Challenger was nothing but a fraud* and a liar.

There was a great roar from the students. 'Here he is! Professor Challenger!'

A huge man swaggered onto the platform. He had an enormous bull-like head, and a long, black rippling beard. He didn't seem at all afraid of the jeering audience. He fixed them with steely eyes. There was something masterful about that gaze. Immediately, silence fell.

'There is a plateau* in South America,' the professor thundered, 'a few days trek from the great river Amazon,*

where prehistoric creatures still survive.'

'Tosh!' called a student.

'Bosh!' yelled another.

Slowly, the professor's great bull head swung round. His eyes blazed into

the crowd. 'Who said that?' he roared, clenching his fists as if ready to fight all the students at once. No one spoke.

'I have proof!' boomed the professor. 'The plateau has sheer, cliff-like walls. I was unable to climb to the top. But I did manage to photograph one of the creatures.'

'Let us see your photograph then,' came the quiet, scornful voice of a professor next to me.

'Aah, Professor Summerlee,' said Challenger,

'my old enemy. I knew you'd be here.'

Challenger held up a blurred grey photograph. Even though I was in the front row, I could hardly make it out.

'It looks like a giant bat to me,' said Summerlee.

The students laughed.

Professor Challenger's face went red as a tomato. His beard was bristling. He looked ready to explode with rage. 'Professor Summerlee!' he bellowed. 'Your brain is as small as a walnut! Any fool can see that it is a pterodactyl!* And there are other prehistoric creatures living up on that plateau. I bet my life on it!'

'But we are scientists,' came Professor Summerlee's quiet, dry voice again. 'We need better proof than this.'

'At the foot of the cliffs,' said Challenger, 'I found a giant bone. It is from something that died quite recently.'

He showed the bone to us, still with shreds of flesh stuck to it. 'I believe it is from a stegosaurus.* It must have been killed when it fell from the plateau.'

'Pah!' scoffed Professor Summerlee. 'All this is pure fantasy! It looks like an elephant bone to me.'

Challenger's reply was drowned out by mocking students. Some trumpeted like elephants. Some waved their arms like trunks. Even some professors were on their feet shouting.

But then Challenger crashed his giant fist onto the table. 'Silence!' he bellowed. 'Professor Summerlee does not believe me!' he roared. 'So I challenge him! I challenge him to go to South America. To see for himself if my story is true!'

Professor Summerlee stood up. The audience fell silent again, waiting to hear his answer.

'I accept your challenge,' he said.

The students cheered wildly.

'It will be a difficult and dangerous mission,' said Challenger. He glared scornfully at the audience. 'Professor Summerlee will need a younger companion. Who is brave enough to go with him?'

I was about to spring to my feet. It was just the kind of adventure I'd been dreaming of.

But I was too late. A tall, wiry, red-haired man had beaten me to it.

'I'm Lord John Roxton,' he said, in a calm, confident voice. 'I've already travelled widely in South America. I'll go with Professor Summerlee.'

I groaned. I thought my chance had gone for ever. But then Challenger said, 'Anyone else?'

This time I leaped from my seat like a rocket. 'My name's Ed Malone!' I cried. 'Reporter on the *Daily Gazette*. I'll go too!'

The cheers were even wilder.

But Professor Challenger roared, 'I hate journalists! They are vile crawling scum!' He rushed to the edge of the platform, his fists ready. 'Come outside and fight!' he roared.

I must admit I lost my temper. I put my fists up too. 'Whenever you're ready, you bully!' I shouted.

There were hoots and howls from the students. 'A fight! A fight!' they chanted.

It was Lord John who calmed the situation. His cool voice cut through the mayhem.* He said, 'We shall need a journalist, to report on what we find.'

'I agree,' said Summerlee.

Challenger was outvoted. He muttered into his beard. But at last he said grudgingly, 'He can come.'

I sat down again. I was trembling with excitement. I thought, 'This is your big chance, Malone. My chance to get the scoop of the century. My chance to be a world-famous reporter!'

Open on 15th July
At 12 O'clock
In Manaos.

CHAPTER 2

The expedition begins

The weeks of getting ready for our South American adventure made me mad with impatience. Would we find the professor's lost world with its amazing prehistoric creatures? Could his story really be true?

Mr McArdle didn't think so. 'Young man,' he said, shaking his head. 'I hope you're not risking your life for nothing.'

At last the great day arrived. Myself, Lord Roxton and Professor Summerlee were about to board the ship that would take us to South America.

Suddenly, we heard a familiar, roaring voice. 'Hey, you there! Wait!' A figure came lumbering up like a bad-tempered bear. It was Professor Challenger.

He thrust a letter into Summerlee's hands. 'There's a town on the Amazon called Manaos,' he told us, in his usual rude, abrupt way. 'When you get there you will open this envelope. In it are my directions for finding the plateau.'

The three of us stood by the gangplank. Would Professor Challenger shake our hands, or wish us good luck? Or even thank us for going to test the truth of his story? There was no chance of that.

Instead he roared out more orders. 'Mind you open that envelope at Manaos! But not before the date and time written on the outside!'

'That man is insufferable!'* muttered Professor Summerlee.

◆◆◆

I won't bore you with our journey to Manaos. It took many weeks, across the Atlantic Ocean and then by river boat up the Amazon.

At least I had plenty of time to get to know my companions.

Professor Summerlee was a tall, stringy fellow. He had a stern, sarcastic manner. He was a dry old stick,* but surprisingly tough. He never once complained or seemed to get tired. Like Mr McArdle, he thought we were on a wild goose chase. He didn't believe for a second that the lost world existed.

'I shall take great satisfaction,' he told us, with his bitter smile, 'in proving Professor Challenger a cheat and a liar.'

17

Lord John Roxton didn't agree. He'd already travelled a great deal around the Amazon. When he talked of it, his quiet manner changed, his cold blue eyes sparkled with enthusiasm. 'I love the place,' he told us. 'It's a dangerous, unknown wilderness. But full of wonders! I wouldn't be surprised if we *did* find a lost world.'

He was a man of action, an adventurer. If there was going to be trouble, I couldn't think of a better person to stand beside me.

We arrived in Manaos, just before the time to open Professor Challenger's envelope.

'Open on 15th July at twelve o'clock,' said Professor Summerlee, reading the instructions. 'Well, it's 15th July.' He checked his watch, 'And now it's twelve o'clock exactly.'

He opened the envelope and took out a piece of paper.

He unfolded it and looked on both sides. Then he gave a great burst of laughter.

'What is it?' I asked, startled. 'What does it say?'

'See for yourselves,' said Professor Summerlee. He shook the paper at us.

'Why, it's nothing but a blank sheet!' said Lord Roxton.

There were no directions to the plateau. Nothing written on the paper at all.

'It proves what I've said all along,' said Summerlee. 'That Challenger is nothing but a shameless fraud. His entire story is an invention!'

At that very moment, a dark shadow fell across the doorway. An arrogant voice boomed, 'May I come in?'

'Professor Challenger!' I gasped.

He came swaggering in, his hands in his pockets, as if he'd just strolled up the street. For once, his great bull head had lost its fierce expression. He beamed at us. He seemed very pleased with himself.

'What are you doing here?' demanded Professor Summerlee, in his sternest voice. 'You were supposed to stay in England.'

'I've come to take charge of the expedition, of course! I shall lead you to the plateau myself. We start at dawn tomorrow!'

'I *told* you the man was insufferable,' muttered Professor Summerlee, under his breath.

CHAPTER 3

Into the unknown

The next day we left Manaos. First we travelled along the Amazon by steamship.* Then we hired a canoe from a village. We packed it with all our stores. Then we set off again with two men from the village paddling.

'Now,' I thought, 'we are really setting out into the unknown.'

We turned off the wide river onto a smaller stream. It was hard going. Every time we met rapids we had to carry the canoe through the forest to calmer water.

Great trees met high over our heads, almost shutting out the sun. Plants writhed and twisted upwards, trying to catch its rays. From the dark bushes on the banks we heard scuttlings,

rustlings. Once, I saw the flash of golden eyes.

It was the creepiest place. But the two professors didn't seem to notice. They were too busy squabbling like children. They couldn't agree about anything.

In the distance, we heard a throbbing beat.

'War drums,' said Lord John carelessly. 'I've heard them before.'

The sound made my skin crawl. *We will kill you if we can,* they seemed to be saying. *We will kill you if we can.*

Our two paddlers listened and shook with fear. But were the professors scared by that sinister sound? Not a bit of it! They only quarrelled harder.

'Those are the drums of the Miranha* people,' snarled Summerlee.

'I disagree, sir!' said Challenger pompously. 'Any fool knows that is the Amajuaca* tribe!'

On the third day, the stream narrowed to a trickle. Our canoe couldn't go any further. We left it behind, and carrying our stores on our backs, the six of us began trekking into the wilderness.

'We are about nine days walk from the plateau,' declared Challenger.

Summerlee never missed the chance to get in a jibe. '*If* it exists,' he said, with his bitter smile.

We struggled on, sometimes sinking in boggy swamps, sometimes hacking our way through jungle. All the way, we were plagued by clouds of biting, stinging insects.

I saw the two village men muttering together. They had had enough, it seemed, of wading through bogs with two feuding boffins.* I thought, 'Are they planning to run away?' If they did, who could blame them?

But they stayed, perhaps out of fear of that great, bellowing bully, Challenger.

On the ninth day, snakes came writhing towards us from a stinking swamp, hundreds of them, their necks swaying above the reeds.

'Run!' cried Lord John.

We ran until we sank down, gasping for breath. Finally, I lifted my head. And saw that Challenger's great bull head was already lifted. He was staring at something. About a mile away was a long line of high, red cliffs.

'There it is!' bellowed Challenger. 'We have reached the plateau!' He threw a look of triumph at Summerlee. 'I told you!'

We camped that night under those plateau walls. Lord John had shot a rabbit for dinner, and it was roasting on our fire.

The cliffs rose sheer and tall above us. They were impossible to climb. We could see trees on top, but no signs of life at all.

'So where are the prehistoric creatures?' jeered Summerlee. Even though we'd reached the plateau, he was as stubborn as ever. He still refused to believe the professor's story.

Challenger pointed out a tall pyramid of rock, like a church spire. It was as high as the cliffs but stood on its own, ten metres away from the plateau. On its top was a great, spreading tree.

'That was where I photographed the pterodactyl,' he said. 'It was perched on that very tree.'

'Fiddlesticks,' murmured Professor Summerlee.

Suddenly, something swooped out of the starry sky. We heard the swish of leathery wings.

'Look out!' cried Lord John, as he ducked down.

I glimpsed a long snake-like neck, fierce red eyes and a great snapping beak. Then it was gone, and so was our dinner!

A huge flapping shadow rose into the air with the rabbit. For a moment, its monster wings blotted out the moon. Then it vanished over the cliff top above us.

It was all over in a flash. We sat there in stunned silence.

Then came Lord John's voice, as cool and quiet as ever. 'I knew we would see wonders,' he said.

'But did you see its teeth?' I spluttered. 'The beak had *teeth* in it, rows of them, razor sharp! That was a pterodactyl, I'd bet on it!'

At last, Professor Summerlee spoke. His voice wasn't sneering this time. It trembled with emotion. 'Professor Challenger,' he said. 'I must apologise to you. All this time I have doubted your word. I was a fool to do so, for I see now that you were telling the truth.'

'Well said!' murmured Lord John.

But would Professor Challenger think the same? For once, the great man didn't behave badly. He didn't crow, or brag or bellow. With great dignity, he told Professor Summerlee, 'I accept your apology, sir.'

And then, for the first time in their lives, the
two old enemies shook hands.

CHAPTER 4

A bridge to the lost world

Seeing that pterodactyl was incredible! I couldn't help thinking of the headlines when I got back to London: 'ACE REPORTER SEES LIVING DINOSAUR!'

But what other creatures lived on top of the plateau? None of us could wait to find out. But how were we going to get up there?

The next morning we left our camp and hiked around the plateau's base, trying to find a way up its mighty walls.

Lord John was an experienced mountain climber. But even he shook his head and said, 'It can't be done.'

We were hacking through a grove of bamboo, when I saw something white glinting in the grass.

I knelt down to look. 'It's a skull!' I cried, shuddering. I moved some grass aside. 'Here are more bones!'

The villagers cleared more space with their machetes. Then we saw a whole skeleton, laid out at the foot of the cliffs.

'It's most certainly human,' said Professor Summerlee, who didn't seem at all upset by the grisly sight.

I expected Challenger to argue. But he simply said, 'My learned friend is right.'

Lord John knelt down to take a closer look. 'Poor fellow,' he said. 'Every bone in his body is broken.' He stared up the sheer plateau walls. 'It seems he fell, or was pushed, from the top.'

A hush fell over us. We all gazed at the top of the plateau. I felt a chill round my heart. 'If he was chucked off,' I was thinking, 'does that mean there are *people* up there?'

That unknown world above us suddenly seemed much more menacing.

We walked back to camp in silence. The two villagers dropped behind us. They were muttering again, and casting scared glances up at the plateau.

But Challenger wasn't worried. He seemed more eager than ever to find a way up. He stomped along for a moment in silence, stroking his huge black beard in thought. Then he startled us by roaring, 'I've got it!'

'Got what?' asked Lord John, in his calm, cool voice.

Challenger's chest puffed out like a peacock. 'Gentlemen,' he cried, 'you may congratulate me. I have solved our problem. We shall climb the spire of rock!'

I stared up at the spire-shaped tower of rock.
It stood next to the plateau. But there was a
great gap between them, and it was far too wide
to jump.

'But what's the good of that?' I asked. 'Even if
we get to the top of the spire, we still can't get to
the plateau.'

Challenger gave me a condescending* smile, as if to say, 'Young man, do as you're told. Leave the thinking to greater minds.'

So we climbed the spire. The others had done more rock climbing than I had. But my youth and strength made up for my inexperience. Lord John scrambled up like a mountain goat. Even Challenger, that great bear of a man, surprised me by how nimble he was.

Puffing and panting, I hauled myself onto the grassy summit. The two professors and Lord John were already there.

The villagers were following us, urged on by Challenger's bullying roars.

'How interesting,' said Professor Summerlee.

You'd hardly believe the old chap had just made that dangerous climb! He was already examining the tall tree that grew on the summit.

I staggered to my feet. What a breathtaking view! A vast, forested plain lay on all sides. It stretched to a misty blue horizon.

A huge, heavy fist fell on my shoulder. It was Challenger. 'Have you guessed yet,' he asked, 'how we shall cross to the plateau?'

I shook my head. My puzzled face made Challenger shout with laughter.

But Lord John was sharper than me. He spotted it instantly. 'By George!' he cried. 'The tree! We can use it for a bridge!'

'Well done!' bellowed Challenger, as if amazed that our inferior brains* had at last caught up. 'We'll chop the tree down across the gap. And then we shall simply walk across. Why do you think I brought this axe all the way up?'

Lord John and I attacked the tree trunk, taking turns with the axe. Soon there was a loud crack. The tree began to sway.

'It's falling!' cried Lord John.

We leaped aside. But would it fall where we wanted? And would it reach the plateau? For one terrible second, I thought the whole tree would tumble into the chasm. But no! The topmost branches crashed down onto the other side. And there was our bridge to the lost world, ready and waiting.

Challenger, of course, bustled to the front. 'I insist on being first over!'

'Wait,' said Lord John, unstrapping his rifle from his backpack. 'You know about science. But I know about exploring. I'll go first. Who knows what's waiting for us on the plateau?'

Our leader huffed and puffed. He hated taking orders of any kind. But there was something about Lord John's quiet authority that made even the great Challenger obey.

Sir John strolled across, looking casual, as if

he was walking in a London park.

But my stomach was fluttering with excitement and fear. I couldn't help thinking of that broken skeleton.

Challenger, of course, seemed to fear nothing. He practically skipped across that tree bridge.

On the other side, he waved his arms in the air. 'At last! At last!' he cried.

Summerlee followed, crawling across the bridge. I crawled too, my legs shaking. I glanced down once at the dizzying drop. But it made me feel so sick that I dared not look again.

At last, all four of us were on the other side.

'Where are the villagers?' grumbled Challenger. 'They should be up here by now.' We had some food and other things in our backpacks. But the villagers were carrying most of our stores.

'Look!' Summerlee suddenly shouted. We all turned round to watch a strange, colourful bird fly up from the grass.

'I believe it's a parrot,' said Summerlee.

Challenger boomed, 'I disagree! Any fool can see it is a giant hummingbird!'

While they were arguing, from behind us, came a terrifying crash. We all spun round at once. Just in time to see the tree hurtling through space and the villagers scrambling down the side of the spire of rock.

'The scoundrels!' raged Challenger, shaking his fist. 'They've pushed our bridge into the chasm. Why did they do that?'

It seemed obvious to me. They'd been scared out of their wits with war drums, pterodactyls and the skeleton. They just wanted to go home. And they wanted to make sure we couldn't chase them and bring them back. What better way than to trap us on the plateau?

There were no large trees near the edge to make a bridge back. No way down the sheer sides. I must admit, I felt very afraid.

'Trapped,' I was thinking. 'Trapped on this lost world, with no hope of ever getting back!'

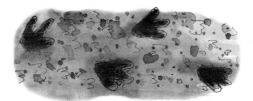

CHAPTER 5

From a dream to a nightmare

'Cheer up, sonny boy,' roared Professor Challenger clapping his great paw on my shoulder. 'There are worst places to be trapped. It's a golden opportunity! Let us go out and explore this new world!'

He was like a child with a marvellous present he can't wait to unwrap. His enthusiasm was catching. I felt my terrors disappear.

'You're right, Professor,' I said eagerly. 'Let's start at once.'

Lord John, practical as ever, reminded us to take care. 'First we must build a camp,' he said. 'A safe place we can retreat to.'

His sharp eyes narrowed as he gazed out over the trees and bushes of the plateau. 'Who knows what's waiting out there? Will it be friend or foe?'

I felt a flicker of fear again. But my excitement took over. 'Whatever it is,' I cried, 'we'll be ready for it!'

'That's the spirit, young fellow!' boomed Challenger.

To make our camp safe, we built a fence of thorn bushes around it. Inside we put our stores – some tins of meat, knives, blankets and a few other things.

I was stacking tins of meat when I noticed something strange on my leg. It was a lump, like a fat, purple grape, stuck to the skin above my sock.

'What's that?' I wondered. I bent down for a closer look. I tried to pick it off. 'Ugh!' I cried, shuddering with horror. The thing had burst between my fingers, squirting blood all over the place.

It was an enormous, swollen insect. It had bitten through my skin and had been drinking my blood!

My cries brought the professors running.

'Most interesting,' said Summerlee, kneeling down to examine what was left of the insect. 'Some kind of tick, I believe. And a giant species, unknown to science.'

'Congratulations, Malone!' boomed Professor Challenger, sarcastically. 'We have just found our first new species on this plateau. And you've squashed it!'

'Filthy creature!' I cried, stomping it into the ground.

Then the professor spoke to me in his most pompous tones. 'My dear young sir,' he said. 'We men of science do not call a tick a "filthy creature". We have wiser and cooler heads. To us, a tick is a beautiful work of nature, to be studied, not stamped on.' He shook his head crossly. 'Now we'll have to find a new specimen.'*

'That'll be easy,' Summerlee told him, 'because one has just crawled down your shirt collar.'

'Aaaargh!' yelled Professor Challenger. He sprang into the air bellowing like a wild bull and tore at his shirt, ripping it open. 'Where is it? Where is the filthy creature?' He danced about, slapping at his neck. 'Have I killed it yet?'

Perhaps Summerlee and I should have helped him. But we couldn't, because we were laughing too much.

The next morning, we left our camp and set out into our new world. Lord John was in the lead, looking out for danger.

We followed a little stream, so we didn't get lost. We pushed our way through chest-high reeds. Great ferns grew around us, higher than our heads.

Summerlee dropped to his knees in the boggy ground. His usually scornful voice was full of wonder. 'Look here!' he cried.

I saw an enormous, three-toed claw track in the mud. A ten-year-old child could have sat in it.

'By George!' marvelled Lord John. 'That bird must be as tall as a tree. And the print is fresh too!' He looked around, gripping his rifle.

'It's not a bird!' said Challenger, beaming with happiness. 'See, there's the print of its forepaw. It's a dinosaur!'

He went bursting through the reeds, following the tracks. As we caught up with him, he turned round and whispered, 'Shhhh!'

All of us ducked down. I peeped out and saw the most extraordinary creatures. There were five of them in a clearing, two adults and three babies. Even the babies were the size of kangaroos.

How shall I describe them? Like giant upright lizards? Like dragons without wings? They had scaly skin that shimmered in the sun, and long, powerful tails. One swish of those tails could knock over a London bus!

They bounded about on their huge back legs. But I didn't feel at all afraid. They seemed like

gentle creatures, pulling down branches from trees and grazing on the leaves.

Then something startled them. They bounded away. We saw their heads above the trees, and then they vanished.

We all stood up. For a moment, none of us spoke.

Then Professor Summerlee whispered, 'Magnificent.'

'Iguanodons,* I believe,' said Challenger, in an awe-stricken voice.

I couldn't help grinning. The two famous professors, like little children, hugged each other with glee! I have never seen them smile so much.

'What will they say at home about this?' I cried. Secretly I thought, 'I'm going to be famous, the most famous reporter in London.'

'They won't believe you,' warned Challenger. 'Just as they didn't believe me.'

'I expect it will seem like a dream to us too, when we get back to London,' said Lord John.

But we were about to go from a dream into a nightmare.

We came out of the woods, still following that little stream, and were crossing a plain scattered with huge rocks.

Suddenly, we heard a strange whistling noise. It was coming from somewhere ahead of us. Then a gabbling* sound filled the air.

Lord John was in front. We saw him run and peer over a line of rocks. What he saw seemed to fascinate him.

Still staring down, he held up his hand, as if to say, 'Be careful!' We crept up and looked down too.

What I saw almost froze me with shock. A huge, shallow bowl in the rock lay below us. It was a nesting place for pterodactyls, hundreds of them!

At the bottom of the bowl was a scummy lake. Around it, adults sat on eggs, their wings wrapped around them like grey shawls, their fierce snaky heads poking up. Young ones crawled about, like giant bats.

From this flapping, croaking mass rose a stink that almost choked us. Then Summerlee, in his eagerness to see, knocked down a small rock.

It rattled into their nesting place. Instantly, the creatures rose up into the air, their great, leathery wings spread wide as they soared over us.

'Make for the woods!' yelled Lord John. 'They're going to attack!'

We ran. But the pterodactyls dived low. Their long necks shot out, their crocodile teeth snapped.

'Agh!' I felt a stab at the back of my neck.

Summerlee gave a cry. I saw blood streaming down his face. The air above us boiled with squawking beaks and clattering wings.

Then Challenger fell as a wing struck him. We helped him up and staggered on.

Now we were among the trees. We were safe!

Looking up, we saw them turn away, soaring high into the sky until they seemed no bigger than bats. Then they were gone, back to their nesting place.

'Most interesting,' said Professor Summerlee, as we limped, battered and bloody, back to camp.

There another shock was waiting for us. Something, or someone, had broken into our camp. They had scattered all our stores about, torn open a tin and eaten the meat inside.

I looked around fearfully. It seemed as if dark shadows were gathering round us. I shivered. Were there eyes in those shadows? I couldn't get over the feeling we were being watched.

Lord John felt the same. He too gazed into the shadows. 'This is not good,' he said, his thin face serious. 'Whoever lives here, seems to know where to find us.'

CHAPTER 6

In deadly peril

Perhaps we should have moved camp. But we were too sick and exhausted after the pterodactyl attack. The bites of those flying monsters must have been poisonous. Professor Summerlee and I both had a fever and we were in great pain all the next day.

When night came, Lord John sat on guard by our camp fence. We three others were sleeping by the fire. Suddenly I sat bolt upright. A terrible cry came from the darkness outside. More came – awful nerve-shattering shrieks of torment. And then a terrible, throaty rumbling roar.

At first, I thought it was my fevered mind. But the screams had woken Challenger and Summerlee too.

'What on earth is that?' I whispered.

The shrieks stopped. But then we heard more awful sounds. A *thump, thump, thump*, like heavy footsteps, was coming closer. Something big was out there, prowling round our camp fence. The beast must have smelled us. It stopped by our gate. We could hear it breathing. Then it snarled.

I felt the hairs rise on the back of my neck. But Lord John kept cool, as always. He made a spy hole in the fence and peered out into the darkness beyond.

'I think I can see it!' he said.

I crawled over and joined him at the spy hole. 'I can see a huge crouching shape, with savage, gleaming eyes,' I told the professors.

Straight away they started discussing what it could be, as if we weren't in deadly peril!

'No doubt a carnivorous* dinosaur,' declared Challenger. 'Perhaps an allosaurus.'*

'Most likely,' said Summerlee in his dry, boffin's voice.

'It's going to jump!' I hissed.

Lord John said, 'If it gets over that fence, we're done for.'

He sprang into action. Grabbing a blazing branch from the fire, he slipped outside. Through the hole in the fence I saw everything. There was a gleam of fangs as the creature rushed forward.

But Lord John didn't hesitate. He ran to meet it and thrust the blazing branch into its face.

I heard a furious roar, caught a glimpse of a warty face, like a giant toad's, dripping with blood. Then the creature turned and plunged back into the forest.

I took my first breath, it seemed, for several minutes.

Lord John came back into camp. 'I thought it wouldn't like fire!' he said.

'That was the bravest thing I've ever seen!' I told him. 'You're a hero!'

'What rubbish!' laughed Lord John, shrugging off my praise. He went back to his guard duty as if nothing had happened.

The next morning we found the reason for those dreadful shrieks in the night. The allosaurus had torn a gentle iguanadon to pieces, and eaten it outside our camp. We were lucky that it hadn't been hungry when it attacked us.

Summerlee was white with horror. 'I believe,' he said, 'we should get down from this plateau as soon as possible. After all, we have done what we came for and proved Challenger's story true.'

'I agree,' I nodded. I had my own reasons for wanting to get back to London. What a story this would make! I'd always wanted the scoop of the century. And now I'd got it.

But Challenger of course, protested. He glared fiercely at us.

'I'm not going back until I have made a map of my lost world. For that, we must explore every corner.'

'But that could take weeks!' complained Summerlee.

Then suddenly I had a brain wave. 'See that tall tree over there?' I said. 'From the top I should be able to see all of the plateau. I'll sketch a map of it in my notebook.'

To my amazement, Challenger didn't argue. He even said, as if surprised, 'Young man, that's a good idea.'

Since we'd started, I'd felt like the baby of the expedition. My companions were older than me, and more experienced. But they couldn't climb trees like I could. At last, I'd found a way of being useful! I couldn't wait to get climbing.

'Take my binoculars,' said Lord John.

I slung them over my shoulder and began scrambling up the trunk. I climbed quickly. Soon, even Challenger's booming voice seemed far away. I swung from branch to branch. It seemed I was climbing to the clouds! But the tree was very tall and there was still a great spread of branches above my head. I pulled myself up higher.

'Aaaargh!' I gave a terrified shriek. I almost fell out of the tree!

A face was peering into mine. It had a low forehead and a jutting jaw. Its tiny, squinting eyes peered at me with malice. Was it ape or human? I was sure it would attack me. But then fear filled its eyes and it crashed down through the tree, swinging from branch to branch. Its whole body was covered with downy red hair.

One last crash and it was gone.

I collapsed over the branch, gasping with relief. I almost started back down. But, after a few minutes, my courage came back. I'd promised Challenger a map of his plateau. Imagine how he'd sneer if I went back without it!

'You must go on,' I told myself sternly.

I met no more ape-men as I climbed to the top and wedged myself between two branches. From up here, I could see the whole plateau – the clearing where the iguanadons grazed, the pterodactyl nesting place. I could also see parts of the plateau we hadn't explored.

In its centre was a great round lake, sparkling in the sun. Through the binoculars I saw strange creatures sunning themselves on its banks. But I couldn't make out what they were.

Then I looked beyond the lake. Through the binoculars, I saw cliffs, with dark holes in them.

'Could they be caves?' I wondered.

I heard an impatient bellow from below. I quickly sketched out a map of what I could see, and scrambled down the tree.

'Did you see it?' I asked breathlessly.

'See what?' asked Lord John.

'The ape-man! He was up in that tree. He must have been watching our camp all this time!'

All three shook their heads. The professors discussed it for a moment in great excitement. Was it more ape than human? Or more human than ape? Could it be the missing link between the two that scientists had been seeking for years?

Then they looked at my map.

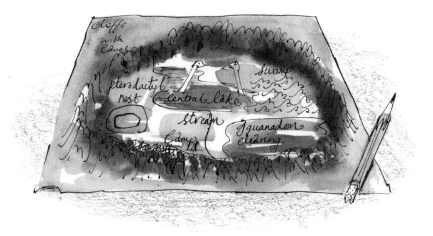

'It's saved us weeks, perhaps months of dangerous exploration,' said Summerlee.

'This is most valuable information,' said Challenger. 'What could those creatures be on the lake shore? Perhaps plesiosaurus,* a swimming dinosaur?'

'Well done, young man,' said Lord John.

Then all three of them shook my hand. I couldn't help feeling a glow of pride. For once, I was the hero of the expedition!

CHAPTER 7

A midnight adventure

That night, Summerlee was on guard duty. I saw his thin, bony figure by the fire. Every so often, his wispy goat's beard wagged as he dozed off.

Challenger and Lord John were asleep, but not me. I was still too excited about my map-making adventure – the ape-man I'd seen, that lake at the centre of the plateau, those caves.

I couldn't help feeling very pleased with myself. Before, I had felt like a boy in the company of men. Now I felt like a real grown-up. I wanted to do something else daring, to win more praise and prove myself to the others once and for all.

'Why don't you go to that lake?' I asked myself. 'And find out more about those mysterious creatures on the shore?'

I could see the others clapping me on the back when I came back, marvelling, 'What, you went out exploring, at night, all alone!'

I could see the headline in my newspaper: TOP REPORTER TAKES MIDNIGHT STROLL IN DINOSAUR FOREST!

'I'll go,' I decided.

It was a very stupid thing to do. My need for praise blinded me. If I'd known then what I know now, I'd never have taken that walk.

I crept past the snoozing Summerlee and plunged into the dark forest, following the little stream, which I was sure would lead me to the central lake.

It was a bright moonlit night, but among the trees, shadows moved. My heart hammered. My head whipped round at every sound. Something scuttled away into the bushes.

I told myself, 'Malone, this is a big mistake.'

My pride had made me do something foolish. But now my pride wouldn't let me go back. Not without completing my mission. So I pushed on through that dreadful forest, with rustlings, howls and all sorts of strange cries around me.

What was that huge crouching shape among the trees? A picture flashed into my mind of the allosaurus, with blood dripping from its jaws. But the shape melted away and I realised it was just my eyes playing tricks.

'Get a grip, Malone,' I told myself sternly.

At last I reached the lake. I seemed to have been walking for hours but my watch said it was only one o'clock in the morning.

But I couldn't afford to waste time. I wanted to explore the lake and be back in camp before dawn.

The lake shone silver in the moonlight. Then I saw ripples. Suddenly a snaky head and neck rose up like a swimming serpent. Then another, then another! Their long necks waved as they glided gracefully through the water. I watched them, fascinated.

The creatures crawled clumsily out onto the bank. They had huge, barrel-shaped bodies and fins like giant seals.

'Plesiosaurs!' I breathed. 'They must be!' How thrilled Challenger would be when I told him. How he'd crow, 'I knew I was right!'*

Then my eyes caught some lights. They were high up, on the cliffs beyond the lake. It was where I'd seen the caves through the binoculars. I stared at them amazed. The lights were red and twinkling. 'Those are fires!' I told myself. 'Fires in the caves. What else could they be?'

And fires meant people. People probably more advanced than the ape-man I'd seen in the tree.

I leaped up, filled with excitement about what I'd learned. I would have liked to explore further, to go around the lake, climb those cliffs and peep into the caves. But I had to get back to camp. And, anyhow, I was mad with impatience to tell the others what I'd found.

Eagerly I set off to follow the stream back. The forest didn't seem as frightening as before. It was peaceful, washed with silver, like a dream landscape. I felt bold and full of confidence. 'Why were you so scared?' I mocked myself.

But then I heard a snarl. At first, I thought I'd imagined it. Then it came again, a low, menacing rumble. I stopped, trembling. The hairs prickled at the back of my neck, my eyes darted round. Where was it coming from?

Over there! I saw an enormous shape in the shadows. It was crouched ready to spring. It had powerful back legs, red gleaming eyes.

'Allosaurus!' my brain shrieked at me.

I took off in a panic, crashing through the woods.

I ran faster than I'd ever run before in my life, until I collapsed in the ferns, my chest burning.

Was it still behind me? I thought for a moment I was safe. Then I saw it, sniffing the ground, following my scent, the scent of fresh meat.

It sprang into a pool of moonlight and I saw its terrible teeth and claws.

I took off again, racing through the forest. It was still behind me, and it was gaining!

The next second I was falling through space, my arms and legs kicking wildly. I heard someone screaming in terror. 'It's me!' I realised, as I hurtled downwards. Then there was a great *thump* and blackness.

When I came to, I felt sick and groggy. What had happened? I was aching and bruised all over. And where was I? It was so dark that I could hardly see a thing. There was a foul smell and my hand was touching something. I pulled it back, disgusted. It was a chunk of rotting meat!

Then I remembered the allosaurus. I staggered to my feet and bumped into a huge stake. As I looked up, moonlight spilled over my face. The stake was sharpened at the top. And I could see that I was in some kind of pit.

'It's a trap,' I thought. 'A dinosaur trap!' The meat and bones around me were their rotting remains.

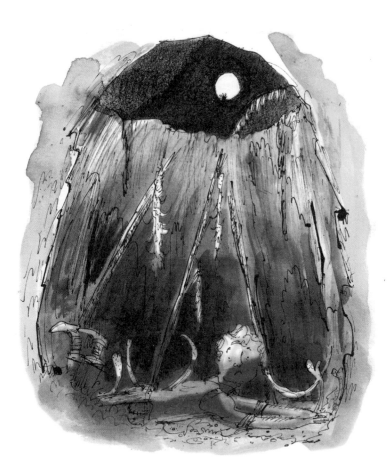

Humans with some cunning and intelligence must have made it. Could it have been the cave dwellers whose fires I'd seen?

But I had more urgent things to think about. Was the allosaurus still on my trail? He could be up there, waiting for me.

A dinosaur couldn't get out of this pit. But a human could. I scrambled up the sides, poked my head over the top and looked around. As far as I could tell, there was no allosaurus. The forest looked peaceful again in the moonlight.

'Anyhow, you can't stay here all night,' I told myself.

So I pulled myself out, found the stream again, and with many nervous looks over my shoulder, I hurried back to camp. I'd still get there before dawn.

I was about a mile away when I heard shouts from the direction of the camp. I stood dead still, my ears straining. Another shrill cry carried though the dark forest. Something was wrong! I forced my poor, aching body into a run.

At last I saw our thorny camp fence in front of me. I shouted out, 'Hey, there!'

No reply. Sick with dread, I stumbled inside. The camp had been smashed up, destroyed, and our things thrown everywhere. My friends had gone.

CHAPTER 8

Prisoners

I panicked. I ran round the camp, shouting, 'Challenger, Summerlee, Lord John!' even though any fool could see there was no one there.

I felt so helpless and alone. I realised how much I'd relied on them – Challenger with his self-confidence, Lord John with his cool courage. How was I going to survive on my own? I slumped down to the ground in despair.

'I'm going to die here!' I moaned, swamped by self-pity.

Then I calmed down a bit and tried to think. 'I'll look for them when it's light,' I decided. I needed rest. I was too exhausted to walk another step.

I lit three fires in the camp and that made me feel braver. I tried to work out what had happened. The camp had been attacked. But by what? Lord John's rifle was still here, but useless, snapped in two. Our cameras and binoculars were smashed. Only the food had been taken. Still puzzling about it, I fell into a restless sleep.

The next thing I knew someone was shaking my shoulder.

'Whaaa?' I croaked. 'What is it?'

A wild-eyed face looked down into mine.

'Lord John!' I cried, fully awake now. His thin face was scratched and bloody, his clothes were torn.

'Quick,' he said, racing off. 'We've got to get out of here! It's the first place the ape-men will look for me!'

I sprang up. 'The ape-men? Did they attack the camp? Where are the professors?'

I followed him, until we stopped, breathless, in a clump of bushes.

'We'll be safe here, for the moment,' said Lord John. Then he told me what had happened.

'Challenger and I were asleep,' he said, 'when the ape-men came leaping down from the trees. Summerlee yelled a warning but it was too late. I managed to grab my rifle, but they tore it from me. Challenger charged at them, bellowing like an angry bull! But there were too many of them. They tied our hands with creepers and marched us off into the jungle. I managed to escape – but the others are in great danger. We must go back and rescue them!'

Lord John grabbed my arm. His eyes glittered with excitement. He seemed to delight in danger. The higher the risk, the more he liked it. 'Come on!' he cried. 'Let's hope we're not too late!'

It was easy to track the ape-men. As they'd dragged their captives along, they'd smashed down grass and bushes. As we got nearer to them, we heard their whoops and chattering cries. We crept through the bushes in silence.

Suddenly, Lord John said, 'Get down!'

Until my dying day I shall never forget what I saw as I peeped out between the ferns.

We were close to the edge of the cliffs, where the trees came to an end. I could see shaggy, red-haired ape creatures, some walking on all fours, some upright. Summerlee was tied to a tree and an ape-man squatted in the branches above him, as if on guard.

'Where's Challenger?' I whispered, fearing the worst.

Then I saw him. His clothes were tattered, his shirt half torn from his hairy chest. But he was not tied up. He was sitting with the largest ape-man, who seemed to be their chief. The ape-man chief was handing him pineapples, in a friendly way, as if to an equal!

And, I must say, at first glance, Professor Challenger and the ape-man looked very alike. The professor had the same squat figure, the same heavy shoulders and long, dangling arms, the same hairiness.

'They look like brothers!' chuckled Lord John. That was just like him, joking in the face of danger. But I was shaking. There were only two of us. How were we going to rescue the professors?

Then, suddenly, two more prisoners were hustled forward from between the trees, their hands tied. They weren't ape creatures, but looked more like humans. There was a girl and a little boy. Both wore animal skins and stone beads. The girl had long dark hair, decorated with brightly coloured feathers.

'Maybe they're cave dwellers?' I wondered.

The little boy was whimpering and terrified.

But if the girl was scared, she hid it well. Her eyes flashed defiance. She held her head high, as proud as a princess.

But then ape-men began dragging the boy towards the cliff edge. The girl cried out, clearly trying to stop them.

With growing horror I saw what they were going to do. I thought of that skeleton, every bone broken, at the bottom of the plateau walls.

'They're going to throw him over the cliff!' I gasped. 'That's what they do with their prisoners!'

But Lord John was already on his feet and running, in a magnificent, desperate, rescue attempt.

'They'll pull him to pieces!' I thought.

Challenger was waving his arms around, shouting, 'No! No!' and trying to make the ape chief stop the killing. But the ape chief grunted and pushed him away, as if they weren't friends any longer.

Then I was up and running too. I saw the ape creatures staring at me, and I thought these were my last moments on Earth.

But suddenly, the edge of the forest seemed to come alive. The ferns shook. The tall grass rippled.

Then, with wild cries, a band of men came running out of the trees. I stopped, bewildered. They were waving flint spears.* They looked very warlike. Like me, Lord John had skidded to a halt, as if he didn't know who to fight first.

But the newcomers weren't after us. Instead, with their stone weapons, they charged at the ape-men. Terrified, the hairy creatures scattered, leaving their prisoners and swinging through the trees to escape.

We could hear their frightened shrieks and howls long after they'd disappeared into the forest.

As the last howl had faded into the distance, I untied Summerlee. He was drooping with shock and weariness, but the brave old boffin still managed to gasp, 'How fascinating! These newcomers must be a Stone Age tribe. I have met ape-men and Stone Age people, all in one day!'

The girl must really have been their princess because her rescuers bowed down low before her and treated her with great respect. She was about to lead them away, but then she seemed to remember us. She turned and beckoned in a friendly way for us to follow with the little boy.

So we tagged on behind, stumbling and blood-streaked. We tramped across a grassy plain and through thorny scrub. Once, we passed a strange pool of boiling mud, coming up through the rocks from deep underground. It bubbled like a magic cauldron. Great blisters of gas burst on its surface.

Summerlee, scientific as ever, said, 'Just as I thought! That proves this whole plateau is an old volcano. There is still some volcanic activity deep underground.'

I thought Challenger would argue. But perhaps he felt guilty for eating pineapples with the ape-man chief, while his fellow professor had been tied up.

'I was trying to tell that ape chief to free you!' he blustered.

'Well, you were taking a long time about it,' said Summerlee, in his dry voice.

'But did you notice,' boomed Challenger, 'what a remarkable creature that ape chief was? How intelligent and handsome!'

'Lord John said you two could have been brothers,' I told him.

Challenger puffed out his chest and seemed to glow with pleasure.

CHAPTER 9

A tunnel to freedom

There isn't much left to tell of our time on the plateau.

The princess and her people did turn out to be cave dwellers. They led us up to their homes, by a steep, narrow staircase cut into the cliff face. There they lived in snug little caverns, safe from ape-men.

We were treated kindly. The cave people fed us and tended our wounds. When we were fit again, we were free to go where we pleased. Lord John and Summerlee and I were determined to find a way down from the plateau. We explored the cave system, with its many tunnels and shafts, hoping that one of them would lead us back to the outside world.

But we had no luck. We always had to turn back because of a dead end or a rock fall.

Only Challenger wandered far from the caves. We often asked him where he'd been. But he only smiled an infuriating secret smile and said, 'To visit my friends, the pterodactyls!'

A little band of cave dwellers always went with him on his mysterious trips. For some reason, they seemed to have taken to the professor. They followed him everywhere.

One day, Challenger told us, 'I have found the answer. I have found a way down from the plateau!'

He led us down to the pool of boiling mud.

'Here is my great invention,' he told us smugly.

Over the bubbling mud, he had spread a huge piece of iguanadon skin. The gas rising from the pool was inflating it, so it swelled up like a huge balloon. It was tied down with ropes, but as the balloon got bigger and bigger, it jerked and tugged at the ropes like a living thing, trying to escape.

'See,' said the professor. 'My balloon will act

like a parachute. We can hold onto the ropes and float down the side of the cliffs.'

'Are you completely mad?' asked Summerlee. 'Do you want to kill us all, you idiot?'

Lord John was more polite. 'It's a very clever idea,' he said. 'But is it strong enough?'

'I'll show you,' roared the professor, glaring at Summerlee for being rude about his invention.

He looped one rope three times round his arms, then slashed at the others with a knife to free the balloon.

Instantly, the gas-filled skin shot into the air, dragging the professor with it. As his feet left the ground, I just had time to throw my arms around his waist. I tried to pull him down, but the balloon was too strong. It whipped me into the air too.

'Help!' I yelled, clinging on desperately to the professor. It felt as if my arms were being ripped from their sockets!

Lord John flung himself at me and grabbed my feet. For a second I felt myself being pulled down. Then the balloon jerked us upwards again.

'I can't hold you!' he gasped.

He was standing on tiptoe. Soon we'd all be whisked into the sky like a string of sausages.

But suddenly there was a crack. The rope had snapped! We tumbled onto the ground in a heap, with coils of rope all over us.

As we staggered to our feet, we saw the balloon soaring away into the blue sky. Soon it was just a speck in the distance.

I was rubbing my sore arms. But the professor was dancing about in triumph. 'Splendid!' he roared. 'That was a total success. All I need is a stronger rope. I shall begin making a second balloon immediately!'

The professor's mad balloon invention made it even more urgent for us to find another way down from the plateau.

It was the princess who gave us a clue. Proudly, she showed us the walls of their caves. They were covered in beautiful paintings of the plateau creatures – leaping gazelle and great, lumbering iguanadons. There were also many strange marks. Was it some kind of primitive* writing?

The princess tried to explain. But we couldn't understand her language.

'It looks like a street map,' I said.

'You are right, young man!' said Summerlee, studying the marks closely. 'I believe this is a map of the entire cave system! And look!' he said excitedly, pointing out a long, sloping line. 'This is a passage we haven't explored. It seems to go much further than the rest...'

'A way down!' said Lord John. 'I'll bet on it!'

And that is how we found our way back. It was clear the cave dwellers didn't want us to leave. And, I admit, I was going to miss them too. They had been good friends to us. Without their help, we couldn't have survived on that plateau. But they were so fond of the professor, we were afraid they might try to stop us.

Lord John, Summerlee, the professor and I set out secretly, just before dawn, before they were all awake. We crept into the long passage with ropes made of creepers and blazing torches to light our way.

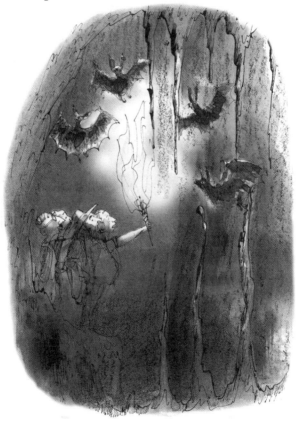

Challenger was loaded down with specimens to take back to London. I tried to help him by carrying one of his boxes. But he snatched it back. 'I'll carry that,' he said rudely.

'Why, what's inside?' I asked him.

'My most precious specimen,' said that maddening man, smiling into his beard.

We passed through bat-filled caves, huge as cathedrals, slithered down shafts and crawled through narrow tunnels.

Then Lord John cried, 'Look, sunlight!'

We came out not far up the plateau walls. It was a simple matter to lower ourselves down on ropes. Challenger stayed until last to make sure his specimens reached the ground safely. We got the box down all right, the one that contained his most precious specimen. But then, disaster struck! He was lowering the rest of his specimens, when the rope broke. His bags fell and were shattered on rocks at the bottom of the cliffs.

I thought the professor would throw a tantrum. Most of his evidence, that he'd worked so hard to collect, was gone. But he amazed us all by keeping calm. 'I still have the specimen that matters,' he said, hugging that mysterious box to his chest.

We rested until the cool of the evening. Then we set out again. I turned around to look at the plateau. It was fiery red in the setting sun. It looked magnificent, mysterious, soaring up into the sky.

'I'll never forget this place,' I murmured to myself. How could I, with all the incredible things we'd seen, all our adventures and all we'd suffered?

'Are you coming, young fellow?' boomed Challenger.

I took one last look. Then turned my back on the lost world for ever, and hurried to catch up with my friends.

CHAPTER 10

Show us your proof!

I shan't bore you with our long journey, by canoe and steamship and ocean liner, back to London.

Instead, I'll skip to the amazing night of the meeting. Two weeks after we arrived home, Challenger spoke once more at the Zoological Institute.

At first, it was just like before. As Challenger appeared, there were the same jeering howls from the students, and the same scornful comments from the professors.

Summerlee, Lord John and I sat listening in silence.

'Fools,' said Summerlee. 'If they would only open their minds...'

But I was secretly very worried. Why should anyone believe Challenger when we had no evidence? His specimens had been smashed to bits on the rocks. Only one box had survived. And that was on the table beside him. I still had no idea what was in it. He'd guarded it jealously on the long journey back to England and wouldn't let any of us near it.

Challenger glared at the audience. They all quietened down when he began to speak. And soon you could have heard a pin drop, as he thrilled them with tales of our adventures, of dinosaurs and ape-man and cave people.

Someone shouted, 'Show us your proof!'

I frowned. 'This is where the trouble starts,' I thought.

'Unfortunately, our cameras were wrecked by ape-men. And almost all my specimens were destroyed in our descent from the plateau,' the professor had to admit.

'That was lucky,' came a jeering voice from the back.

Challenger clenched his fists. He stamped to the front of the stage. Would he lose his temper?

Would he leap down into the audience, fists flying? But, somehow, he carried on.

He told them about the pterodactyls, his particular favourite. He was almost poetic when he described them. Again the audience was spellbound. 'I have seen these fabulous creatures with my own eyes,' he boomed.

'Tosh!' one student dared to shout out.

'Are you calling me a liar?' growled Challenger, his fists clenching again.

Then the student shouted, 'I won't believe it, until I've seen one of these pterodactyls for myself.'

Suddenly, Challenger's mood changed. His fists unclenched. He even began to smile into his beard. He turned to that mysterious box on the table.

'What has he got up his sleeve?' I wondered.

Very slowly, he opened the lid.

'Come on, my pretty,' coaxed Challenger, gazing inside.

A scaly head shot out of the box. It had two fierce, red eyes, a beak and rows of sharp teeth. It was a young pterodactyl!

'I brought it back as an egg,' Challenger explained. 'It hatched out in my flat here in London.'

But no one was listening. There were shouts of horror. Some people ran for the exits.

'Do you believe me now?' Challenger roared triumphantly at the panicking crowd. *Do you believe me now?*

The creature flapped its huge leathery wings. Challenger made a grab for its legs – but too late!

With a great swoosh, it rose above our heads and swooped around the hall. People ducked, some dived under seats.

'The window! Close the window!' bellowed
Challenger. Lord John rushed to do it, but
even he couldn't fight his way through the
struggling mob.

The young pterodactyl sailed out of the open window, free at last.

We all rushed outside, Summerlee, Lord John, Challenger and I.

The last we saw of the pterodactyl, it was flapping away over London, like a monstrous bat. Would it find its way by instinct, back to its lost world home?

I shall always believe that it did.

Arthur Conan Doyle
(born 1859, died 1930)

Arthur Doyle was born in Scotland, to an English father and an Irish mother. He added the middle name 'Conan' to his surname later on, but it is not known why. His mother played an important part in his interest in literature, as she often told him stories. He said, 'In my early childhood, as far as I can remember anything at all, the vivid stories she would tell me stand out so clearly that they obscure the real facts of my life.'

Conan Doyle studied medicine at Edinburgh University and also began writing short stories, the first of which was published when he was 19. After university, he worked as a ship's doctor and practised medicine in Plymouth. But as his practice wasn't very successful, he started writing stories again to fill in time while waiting for patients.

He is best known for his highly popular Sherlock Holmes stories, which have been translated into more than 50 languages. There are 56 short stories and four novels featuring Sherlock Holmes.

Best known works
Collections of short stories
The Adventures of Sherlock Holmes
The Case-Book of Sherlock Holmes

Novels
The Hound of the Baskervilles
A Study in Scarlet

Susan Gates

Before Susan became a full-time writer she taught in secondary schools in Africa and England. She has three children and lives in County Durham.

Susan says, 'I have lost count of the number of children's books I have written – but I think it must be getting close to one hundred!'

Susan adapted *The Lost World* because she believes it's a brilliant adventure story. 'I think it has everything – dinosaurs, daring deeds, nail-biting tension and great characters like Professor Challenger. *The Lost World* is also based on a real place – a plateau called Monte Roraima in South America. Although no one has discovered dinosaurs there (yet!), it has species living on the plateau that are found nowhere else on Earth.'

Notes about this book

This adventure story, published in 1912, was the 'boy's book' that Arthur Conan Doyle had an ambition to write. It tells of an expedition to an isolated area of South America, where one of the main characters in the story, Professor Challenger, claims that he has discovered living dinosaurs, previously thought to have been extinct.

Doyle based some of the main characters in the story on real people known to him. The two professors in the story were based on two of his professors at Edinburgh University, where he was studying medicine – William Rutherford and Robert Christison.

Interestingly, the descriptions of some of the dinosaurs in the book are inaccurate, mostly in the matter of size. The allosaurus, for example, is much smaller in the book than it was in real life.

The Lost World has been adapted for film, television and radio many times.

Page 5
* **scoop** A sensational news story that has not yet been published in any other newspaper or magazine.

Page 6
* **zoological** Zoology is the scientific study of animals.

Page 9
* **fraud** Someone who deliberately tries to hide the truth for personal gain.

*plateau A flat area of high land.
*Amazon The world's biggest river, and the huge area of rainforest surrounding it, in South America.

Page 11
*pterodactyl A flying reptile with a huge wingspan.
*stegosaurus A large, heavily-built herbivorous (plant-eating) dinosaur, with tail spikes and back plates.

Page 14
*mayhem Chaos or disorder.

Page 16
*insufferable Very difficult to put up with.

Page 17
*dry old stick Someone who doesn't display emotion and always acts and speaks in a logical and formal way.

Page 21
*steamship A ship which is powered by steam heated in a boiler by burning coal or oil.

Page 23
*Miranha people/Amajuaca tribe The Amazon jungle contains a large number of different tribes, some of which may consist of only a few hundred people.

Page 24
*boffins People whose main interest is in science.

Page 34
*condescending To be condescending is to treat somebody else as if they are very stupid.

Page 35
* **inferior brains** A way of describing someone who is less clever than others.

Page 42
* **specimen** When scientists collect samples of new discoveries (e.g. plants) they are called specimens.

Page 45
* **iguanodons** Large herbivorous (plant-eating) dinosaurs.
* **gabbling** Speaking so fast and excitedly that it is hard to understand what is being said.

Page 51
* **carnivorous** Meat-eating.
* **allosaurus** A very large carnivorous dinosaur that walked on two legs.

Page 58
* **plesiosaurus** A large marine reptile with a small head, a broad turtle-like body, a short tail and two pairs of large, long paddles.

Page 61
* **'How he'd crow…'** To crow is to publicly display your triumph when you are right and someone else is wrong.

Page 73
* **flint spears** Wooden spears with a pointed head made of sharpened stone. Flint is a type of stone that was used by Stone Age people for tools and weapons.

Page 80
* **primitive** From a very early time period in history.